KU-178-855

Higher

Physical Education

2002 Exam

2003 Exam

2004 Exam

2005 SQP

2005 Exam

Leckie×Leckie

© Scottish Qualifications Authority

All rights reserved. Copying prohibited. No part of this publication may be reproduced, stored in a retrieval system, or transmitted in any form or by any means, electronic, mechanical, photocopying, recording or otherwise.

First exam published in 2002.

Published by Leckie & Leckie, 8 Whitehill Terrace, St. Andrews, Scotland KY16 8RN tel: 01334 475656 fax: 01334 477392
enquiries@leckieandleckie.co.uk www.leckieandleckie.co.uk

ISBN 1-84372-349-2

A CIP Catalogue record for this book is available from the British Library.

Printed in Scotland by Scotprint.

Leckie & Leckie is a division of Granada Learning Limited, part of ITV plc.

Acknowledgements

Leckie & Leckie is grateful to the copyright holders, as credited at the back of the book, for permission to use their material.
Every effort has been made to trace the copyright holders and to obtain their permission for the use of copyright material.
Leckie & Leckie will gladly receive information enabling them to rectify any error or omission in subsequent editions.

2002 | Higher

[BLANK]

X068/301

NATIONAL
QUALIFICATIONS
2002

TUESDAY, 4 JUNE
1.00 PM – 3.30 PM

PHYSICAL
EDUCATION
HIGHER
Analysis of Performance

Candidates should attempt **three** questions, each chosen from a different area.

SCOTTISH
QUALIFICATIONS
AUTHORITY

©

AREA 1: PERFORMANCE APPRECIATION

Question 1

(a) Outline the **range of qualities** you would expect a **model performer** to demonstrate in **one** selected activity.

6

(b) Explain how the use of an appropriate model (or models) of performance helped to establish your **training priorities**. Give **two examples** of training priorities you have identified through the use of your model(s).

5

(c) **Mental factors** can influence performance. Discuss how mental factors have influenced your performance in **two different ways**.

5

(d) Explain how your **training** helps you cope with the **mental pressures** you may experience while performing.

4

(20)

Question 2

Good performers possess abilities of different kinds.

(a) **With reference to the above statement**, describe, in detail, **your** performance in **one** activity.

6

(b) With reference to your description in Part (a), discuss **one long-term goal** which you have for your performance in this activity.

4

(c) Explain how you would use **shorter-term goals** to help you make progress toward the **long-term goal** you have identified in Part (b). Give specific examples.

6

(d) Performance can be **monitored** using different methods. Select **one** method you used and discuss why it was **helpful** in the development of your performance.

4

(20)

Question 3

(a) Choose **one** activity. Describe, in detail, the **overall nature** and **demands** of quality performance in your chosen activity.

6

(b) Describe **how you collected** data about **different aspects** of your performance in the selected activity.

4

(c) **What information** about your strengths, weaknesses and development needs were you able to gain from the data you collected?

6

(d) Special qualities like **imagination** or **creativity** can influence performance. Describe **one** performance situation where you have shown imagination or creativity. Explain how the **quality** of your performance was affected.

4

(20)

AREA 2: PREPARATION OF THE BODY

Marks

Question 4

Choose **one** activity.

(a) Describe, in detail, the **specific fitness demands** required for successful performance in this activity.　　6

(b) Describe **two different methods** you used to collect information about your fitness in relation to the specific demands identified in Part (a).　　4

(c) Explain why it is important to collect information on **your** fitness **before** planning a training programme.　　4

(d) Having collected information about your fitness, discuss **how you applied** the **principles of training** when planning and implementing your training programme.　Give examples to support your answer.　　6

　　(20)

Question 5

(a) Choose **one** activity.　Describe your level of performance in this activity in relation to **one** of the following:

physical fitness
skill-related fitness
mental fitness.　　5

(b) Discuss the importance of the selected **type of fitness** for effective performance in the activity.　　5

(c) Discuss why it is important to consider **phases of training** when planning your training programme.　　4

(d) With reference to **one** of the phases of training, give details of the **training programme** you used to develop your fitness for your chosen activity.　　6

　　(20)

[Area 2 continues on *Page four*

AREA 2: PREPARATION OF THE BODY (continued)

Question 6

Fitness can be developed through different approaches to training.

(a) Choose **one** activity.

Select **one** of the following:

> **training within the activity**
> **training outwith the activity**
> **combination of both.**

Discuss why the approach selected was appropriate for developing **your** **fitness**.

6

(b) Describe, in detail, **one** training session where you used the approach chosen in Part (a) to develop the fitness requirements for your selected activity.

6

(c) As you carried out your training programme you will have **monitored** **your progress**. Discuss the part that monitoring played in developing your programme.

4

(d) Explain the effect that training had on your **overall performance**. Give specific examples to support your answer.

4

(20)

AREA 3: SKILLS AND TECHNIQUE

Marks

Question 7

(a) Choose **one** activity. Describe some of the **fundamental** skills and/or techniques you need to perform well in this activity. **4**

(b) Describe what you did to **obtain information** about your strengths and weaknesses when applying these skills/techniques in a **full performance situation**. **4**

(c) Choose **two** of the skills or techniques described in Part (a). Discuss **your** strengths and weaknesses when you are applying them in **full performance situations**. **6**

(d) When preparing to meet the demands of the **full performance situation** explain how you ensured that the **methods of practice** that you used were appropriate. Give examples to illustrate your answer. **6**

(20)

Question 8

(a) Choose an activity and from it **one** skill or technique which you analysed through using:

- **mechanical analysis**
  or
- **movement analysis**
  or
- **consideration of quality.**

Describe, in detail, the **specific criteria** you used when analysing the skill or technique through **one** of the methods of analysis. **4**

(b) Describe, in detail, the information about **your performance** of the chosen skill or technique, that you were able to obtain from the analysis carried out in Part (a). **6**

(c) Explain how you used **this information** to help you plan a programme of **progressive practices**. **6**

(d) Discuss how your **whole performance** was affected as a result of your practice programme. **4**

(20)

Question 9

(a) Choose **one** activity. Describe the **ways** you have learned skills or developed technique at **two different stages** in your performance development. Give an example for each stage. **8**

(b) Discuss the **principles of effective practice** that you considered to ensure your practice was successful. **6**

(c) Discuss the significance of **one** of the following in relation to learning skills or developing technique:

- **motivation**
- **concentration**
- **feedback.** **6**

(20)

AREA 4: STRUCTURES, STRATEGIES AND COMPOSITION

Marks

Question 10

(a) From an activity of your choice, describe **two** Structures, Strategies or Compositions you have used.

6

(b) (i) Choose **one** of the Structures, Strategies or Compositions described in Part (a). Describe the **advantages** that can be gained when applying this particular Structure, Strategy or Composition.

4

(ii) Describe the **weaknesses** that have to be taken into account when applying this particular Structure, Strategy, or Composition.

4

(c) What **adaptations** within the chosen Structure, Strategy or Composition would you consider in order to maximize its **potential strengths** and minimize its **potential weaknesses**?

6

(20)

Question 11

(a) Describe a Structure, Strategy, or Composition you have used in an activity of your choice.

4

(b) Choose **two** from the list below:

- strengths and weaknesses
- relevant systems of play
- developing motifs
- creativity and improvisation
- width, depth and mobility
- linking space, body actions and dynamics
- co-operation
- communication
- timing and precision
- mood

Explain, in detail, why **each** is important when applying the Structure, Strategy or Composition described in Part (a).

6

(c) Describe a situation where it was necessary to **adapt** your Structure, Strategy or Composition. Explain, in detail, the **decision(s) you took** in order to adapt your Structure, Strategy or Composition.

6

(d) As a result of the decision(s) you made, explain the effects this had on your **overall performance** in the chosen Structure, Strategy or Composition.

4

(20)

AREA 4: STRUCTURES, STRATEGIES AND COMPOSITION (continued)   *Marks*

Question 12

(a) Select a Structure, Strategy or Composition. Discuss the **strengths a performer or performers** require to successfully implement this Structure, Strategy or Composition.   **6**

(b) Describe a **significant problem** you experienced when performing within this Structure, Strategy or Composition.   **4**

(c) Describe, in detail, a programme of work which **addressed the problem** described in Part (b).   **6**

(d) On completion of your programme of work explain, **how you would evaluate** whether improvement had taken place in your performance within the chosen Structure, Strategy or Composition.   **4**

     (20)

[END OF QUESTION PAPER]

[BLANK PAGE]

2003 | Higher

[BLANK]

X068/301

NATIONAL
QUALIFICATIONS
2003

TUESDAY, 3 JUNE
1.00 PM – 3.30 PM

PHYSICAL
EDUCATION
HIGHER
Analysis of Performance

Candidates should attempt **three** questions, each chosen from a different area.

SCOTTISH
QUALIFICATIONS
AUTHORITY

AREA 1: PERFORMANCE APPRECIATION

Marks

Question 1

(*a*) A **quality** performance fully embraces the **nature** and **demands** of an activity. Choose **an** activity and describe the features you would expect to see in such a performance.　　**6**

(*b*) Describe **your** performance **in comparison to** the performance you have outlined in Part (*a*).　　**4**

(*c*) Describe and explain your **thoughts** and **feelings**:

   (i)　when you were **performing well**;

   (ii)　when your performance was **disappointing** you.　　**4**

   (You may use one or more activities to answer Parts (i) and (ii).)

(*d*) **Other people, and external factors, can influence the quality of performances we give.**

   Discuss how another person, other people and external factors have influenced performances you have given. (You may use one or more activities to illustrate your answer.)　　**6**

(20)

Question 2

(*a*) With reference to **two** of the performance qualities listed below, discuss, for **each**, the **strengths** and **weaknesses** of your performance in **one** activity.

- **technical**
- **physical**
- **personal**
- **special**　　**6**

(*b*) Describe the **methods** you used to **identify** the strengths and weaknesses discussed in Part (*a*).　　**4**

(*c*) Discuss how you used the information you obtained to plan your performance training.　　**4**

(*d*) With reference to **your** performance(s) in **one** activity, describe:

   (i)　what you did to **make the most of** your performance **strengths**;

   (ii)　what you did to **reduce the effect of** your performance **weaknesses**.　　**6**

(20)

AREA 1: PERFORMANCE APPRECIATION (continued)

Marks

Question 3

(a) Describe how **mental factors** influence both your **training** and your **performance**.

4

(b) The study of **model performance** can be helpful in the development of **your whole performance**. Discuss how you used the study of model performance to help you develop **different aspects** of your own performance.

6

(c) Outline **a goal** you had for your **whole performance** in **one** activity. Describe, in detail, the **steps you took** to try to achieve this goal.

6

(d) Discuss the effectiveness of the steps you took to achieve your goal.

4

(20)

[Turn over

AREA 2: PREPARATION OF THE BODY

Marks

Question 4

(a) Choose **one** activity. With reference to **your own fitness levels**, discuss the specific fitness demands of this activity.

6

(b) With reference to **two** of the fitness demands you identified in Part (a), describe, briefly, the **methods** you used to assess your fitness.

4

(c) Discuss how your training was **planned** over a **period of time** to ensure your fitness was **maintained** and **improved**.

6

(d) Discuss some of the **indicators** that told you about the **effectiveness of your training** in relation to your **whole performance**.

4

(20)

Question 5

(a) Choose **an** activity and **two** aspects of **physical fitness** that are important in the activity. Explain why these aspects of fitness are important for **effective** performance.

6

(b) Choose **one** aspect of **skill-related fitness** and discuss how **it** affects the way you perform in **an** activity.

4

(c) Explain **why** it is important to be **mentally prepared** to perform successfully.

4

(d) Describe the **training methods** you used to meet your needs for **two different types** of fitness (physical, skill-related or mental). (You may use different activities for each type of fitness chosen.)

6

(20)

Question 6

(a) Choose **one** activity. Discuss the **range** of fitness demands required for effective performance in this activity.

6

(b) Choose **one** of the fitness demands discussed in Part (a). Describe, in detail, **one** training session designed to develop this aspect of fitness.

6

(c) Discuss the **effectiveness** of the training method(s) you used.

4

(d) Describe how **target setting** and the **monitoring of training** helped you make progress towards your fitness goals.

4

(20)

AREA 3: SKILLS AND TECHNIQUE

Marks

Question 7

(a) Choose an activity and **two** methods you have used to **obtain information** about your skills or technique. Explain why you consider **each** method to be appropriate.

4

(b) As a result of **analysing** the information you obtained, describe, in detail, an aspect(s) of your skills or technique that required to be developed.

6

(c) Outline a skills or technique development programme you used to improve the aspect(s) identified in Part (b).

6

(d) It is important to **monitor the effectiveness** of your development programme. Explain why this monitoring process is necessary.

4

(20)

Question 8

(a) Choose an activity. Give a detailed description of a **complex** skill or technique, identifying the features which make it difficult to perform.

4

(b) Describe, in detail, **two** different **methods of practice** you used to develop the **complex** skill or technique described in Part (a). Explain why **each** method of practice was appropriate.

6

(c) Discuss the **principles of effective practice** you applied when using the methods of practice identified in Part (b).

6

(d) Following a period of practice, discuss why your performance may not always be effective when applying **this** skill or technique in **whole performance** situations.

4

(20)

Question 9

(a) Choose an activity. Describe, in detail, a skill or technique which is a **strength** in your performance. Give examples of how you use this strength in your performance.

6

(b) Describe the **method(s) of analysis** you used to identify this skill or technique as a strength in your performance.

4

(c) When **refining** the skill or technique you described in Part (a), discuss the **methods of practice** which you considered to be the most appropriate.

6

(d) Choose **one** of the factors below.

- **motivation**
- **concentration**
- **feedback**

Discuss how **this** factor helped you **maintain or develop** your performance strength as described in Part (a).

4

(20)

[Turn over

AREA 4: STRUCTURES, STRATEGIES AND COMPOSITION

Marks

Question 10

(a) Choose an activity and a structure, strategy or composition you have used. Describe, briefly, **two strengths** and **two weaknesses** that affected your performance when applying this structure, strategy or composition.　　**6**

(b) With reference to your **performance strengths**, discuss why you are **suited to the demands** of performance within this structure, strategy or composition.　　**5**

(c) Describe, in detail, what you did to **address your weaknesses** within this structure, strategy or composition.　　**5**

(d) As a result of the action(s) you took, discuss what you were able to **do more effectively** within the selected structure, strategy or composition.　　**4**

(20)

Question 11

(a) Choose an activity. Describe, in detail, **two** structures, strategies or compositions, **one** which you consider to be your **first choice** and **one** which you consider to be your **alternative** or **second choice**.　　**6**

(b) Explain why you favour your **first choice** structure, strategy or composition.　　**4**

(c) When using your first choice structure, strategy or composition, describe a situation which put you **under pressure**. Explain why your **alternative** structure, strategy or composition was more effective in dealing with this pressure.　　**6**

(d) As you applied your **alternative** structure, strategy or composition, discuss the importance of continually **monitoring** its effectiveness.　　**4**

(20)

Question 12

(a) Describe some of the **problems you encountered** when applying a chosen structure, strategy or composition in an activity of your choice.　　**4**

(b) Explain, in detail, the changes you made to **solve the problems** you described in Part (a).　　**6**

(c) Choose **one** of the factors listed below.

- **strategic or compositional awareness**
- **being creative or able to improvise**
- **dealing with pressure**

Discuss how an awareness of this factor helped you to **make decisions** when applying the structure, strategy or composition selected in Part (a).　　**6**

(d) Describe how you would **evaluate the effectiveness** of your performance in relation to the factor selected in Part (c).　　**4**

(20)

[END OF QUESTION PAPER]

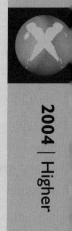

[BLANK]

X068/301

NATIONAL QUALIFICATIONS 2004	THURSDAY, 3 JUNE 1.00 PM – 3.30 PM	PHYSICAL EDUCATION HIGHER Analysis of Performance

Candidates should attempt **three** questions, each chosen from a different area.

SCOTTISH
QUALIFICATIONS
AUTHORITY

©

AREA 1: PERFORMANCE APPRECIATION

Marks

Question 1

(a) Choose **three** of the qualities listed below and describe the extent to which they can be observed in your current performance. You may use **one or more** activities to answer this question.

Imagination   Consistency   Accuracy   Expression   Refinement

Power   Determination   Fluency   Creativity

6

(b) Describe a method(s) you used to **obtain and record information** about your performance qualities.

4

(c) Discuss how you organised your performance training to allow for the development of **any two** of the qualities listed in Part (a). Give specific examples of work undertaken.

6

(d) Discuss your **long term goals** for the development of the qualities you selected in Part (c).

4

(20)

Question 2

Performance can present different **levels of demand** according to the nature of particular performance challenges.

(a) Choose **one** activity. Describe **one** whole performance situation where you were able to cope easily. Explain why it was easy for you to cope.

4

(b) From the **same activity**, describe a whole performance situation where you were **pushed to your limits**. Discuss, in detail, the difficulties you experienced and the nature of the challenge which put you under this pressure.

6

(c) Discuss how you planned to become **more effective** in demanding performance situations.

4

(d) The level of **confidence** you have in your own abilities affects the **way** you perform.

Discuss this statement with reference to **your whole performance** in **two** different performance situations. Choose **one situation** where you **felt confident** in your abilities and a **second situation** where you **lacked confidence** in your abilities.

6

(20)

AREA 1: PERFORMANCE APPRECIATION (continued)

Marks

Question 3

(*a*) In trying to reach your **whole performance goal**, you will have had different types of **training goals**.

In an activity of your choice:

   (i) describe a **whole performance goal** you tried to achieve;

  (ii) describe **two** training goals you used to develop **different areas** of your performance.   (Your two training goals should relate to your whole performance goal.)   **6**

(*b*) Discuss how you used one or more **model performers** to help you establish your goal(s).   **4**

(*c*) Describe, in detail, the **range of abilities** you would expect to see in a model performance of your chosen activity.   **5**

(*d*) With reference to the **range of abilities** described in Part (*c*), discuss the strengths and weaknesses in **your** performance.   **5**

        (20)

[Turn over

AREA 2: PREPARATION OF THE BODY

Marks

Question 4

Choose **one** activity.

(a) Select **two types** of fitness from the list below. Describe, briefly, the method(s) you used to collect data about each type.

- **physical fitness**
- **skill-related fitness**
- **mental fitness**

4

(b) (i) For each **type** of fitness selected, discuss what your data told you about your fitness levels.

4

(ii) Discuss how these fitness levels affected your whole performance.

4

(c) Discuss how you **planned training** to address the needs you identified for **both types** of fitness. Give specific details of how the programme was implemented.

8

(20)

Question 5

(a) Successful performance in any activity demands **some aspects of all** of these **types of fitness**.

- **physical fitness**
- **skill-related fitness**
- **mental fitness**

Choose **one activity**. Discuss the importance of **one aspect** of **each** of these **types of fitness** that you needed for successful performance.

6

(b) Choose **one** of the **aspects** discussed in Part (a). For the aspect chosen, describe how you assessed your fitness in a **whole performance situation**. Describe, briefly, the main findings of this assessment.

4

(c) Choose **another** of the **aspects** you discussed in Part (a). Describe how you assessed your fitness for **this** aspect **outwith** a **whole performance situation**. Describe, briefly, the main findings of this assessment.

4

(d) Discuss how you applied the **principles of training** when planning a programme to meet your identified fitness needs.

6

(20)

AREA 2: PREPARATION OF THE BODY (continued)

Marks

Question 6

In trying to achieve your performance goals, you will have gone through different phases of training lasting for different periods of time.

Training time span		
Preparatory training phase	Competition or Performance phase of training	Transition phase

(a) Choose **one** of the phases of training shown above and describe, in detail, the training you did **during this phase**.

6

(b) Choose **another** of the phases of training. Explain why your fitness training was **different** in this phase. Give specific examples of the differences.

6

(c) Discuss the importance of **monitoring** your training during its different phases. Give a brief description of the methods you used.

4

(d) Throughout the different phases of your training you will have set goals. Discuss the **factors** you considered when **setting your training goals**.

4

(20)

[Turn over

AREA 3: SKILLS AND TECHNIQUE

Marks

Question 7

Mechanical analysis, movement analysis and consideration of quality are regarded as being useful methods when analysing performance in the area of skills and technique.

(a) Choose an activity. Describe, in detail, the **method of analysis** you used to gather information about your performance of **one** selected skill or technique. **4**

(b) Explain why you considered this method of analysis to be appropriate to the activity and the skill or technique involved. **4**

(c) As you attempted to develop your performance of the skill or technique selected in Part (a), you will have used different **methods of practice**. Describe the methods of practice you used. **6**

(d) Discuss why the methods of practice you used were appropriate. Make specific reference to the ways they helped you to develop the skill or technique involved. **6**

(20)

Question 8

(a) Choose an activity. Describe, in detail, **one** skill or technique you have attempted to develop. **4**

(b) Describe a practice situation which allowed you to **refine** the skill or technique **and simultaneously** improve your **decision making**. Explain why this practice situation was effective in helping you develop your whole performance. **6**

(c) Discuss the **range of information** you need to consider to allow you to **make effective decisions** in your whole performance. **6**

(d) How did you assess any improvement in your ability to make effective decisions? **4**

(20)

Question 9

When learning or developing skills or technique, it is important that you use practices that are appropriate to your stage of learning.

Choose an activity and a skill or technique.

(a) Describe **methods of practice** that you used at the **cognitive (preparation) stage of learning**. Explain why these methods were appropriate. **5**

(b) Describe the methods of practice that you used to consolidate your skills or technique at the **associative (practice) stage of learning**. Explain why these methods were appropriate. **5**

(c) Discuss the importance of **feedback** when learning and developing skills/technique at **each** of the the above stages of learning. **6**

(d) Discuss **one** other factor that you considered to be important when learning and developing skills or technique. **4**

(20)

AREA 4: STRUCTURES, STRATEGIES AND COMPOSITION   *Marks*

Question 10

(a) Describe a structure, strategy or composition that you have used in an activity of your choice. Describe **your role** as you applied this structure, strategy or composition.   **4**

(b) Describe **the method(s)** you used to collect information about the effectiveness of your role as you applied this structure, strategy or composition.   **4**

(c) With reference to the information collected, discuss how your **strengths** and **weaknesses** affected the performance of your role.   **6**

(d) (i) Outline the programme of work that you followed to develop your role in the application of the structure, strategy or composition.   **2**

   (ii) Discuss why this programme was appropriate.   **4**

          (20)

Question 11

(a) Choose an activity. Briefly describe a structure, strategy or composition you have used. Discuss the circumstances where you would choose to use this structure, strategy or composition.   **6**

(b) Describe an **alternative** structure, strategy or composition you have used. Discuss the circumstances where you would choose to use this alternative.   **6**

(c) Choose **one** of the structures, strategies or compositions you have described in Part (a) **or** Part (b). Discuss the importance of **two** of the following to ensure the effective performance of this structure, strategy or composition.

   roles and relationships
   formations
   group and team principles
   tactical or design elements
   choreography and composition   **8**

          (20)

[Area 4 continues on *Page eight*

AREA 4: STRUCTURES, STRATEGIES AND COMPOSITION (continued)   *Marks*

Question 12

(a) Choose an activity. Describe, in detail, **one** structure, strategy or composition you have used.   **4**

(b) Discuss the **strengths** a performer or performers require in order to implement this structure, strategy or composition successfully. Give examples of why these strengths are essential.   **6**

(c) Describe, in detail, a **programme of work** you used to develop the **strengths** which a performer or performers require to apply this structure, strategy or composition.   **6**

(d) Identify **one limitation** you were aware of when applying your chosen structure, strategy or composition. Explain what you did to **minimise** the effect of this limitation.   **4**

(20)

[END OF QUESTION PAPER]

Dear Student

In 2005 the format of the Higher Physical Education exam was changed. The following Specimen Question Paper and the actual 2005 exam will give you good practice in the new format. However, the previous years' exams in this book will provide just as good revision and exam-practice features.

Here is some information about the new exam format:

The Question Paper
- You can score up to 60 marks.

- You will be allowed 2 hours 30 minutes for this exam.

- It will test your ability to understand and apply your skills and Key Concept knowledge of Analysis and Development of Performance and each Area of Analysis.

- It will be in four sections, one per Area of Analysis

- You will have to answer three questions in total, each chosen from a different section. Within each section there are two questions.

Each question will:
- be worth 20 marks and will be split into four parts

- will be answerable by all candidates in that it will not be specific to any particular activity

- have links between its parts, testing your relevant Key Concepts knowledge and analysis skills

- ask you to use your relevant practical experiences.

In answering the questions, you will need to show your abilities to:
- describe, record and clearly explain features of your performance

- use a range of relevant concepts and knowledge to analyse performance

- apply knowledge and understanding when discussing the design, completion and monitoring of programmes of work that are likely to lead to performance development

- complete an evaluation of the analysis and development process.

Please visit *www.sqa.org.uk* for further details.

[BLANK PAGE]

[C205/SQP233]

Physical Education   Time: 2 hours 30 mins   NATIONAL

Higher   QUALIFICATIONS

Specimen Question Paper

for use in and after 2005

Candidates should attempt **three** questions, **each** chosen from a **different section**.

SCOTTISH
QUALIFICATIONS
AUTHORITY

©

SECTION 1: PERFORMANCE APPRECIATION

Marks

Question 1

Choose **one** activity.

(a) Discuss, both, the **challenges** of this activity for you and the **qualities** you identified as your strengths and development needs.

6

(b) Choose **one** of the **qualities** discussed in Part (a) that was identified as a **development need**.

Describe the extent of the development need and exactly how it was identified.

4

(c) **Awareness of performance weaknesses can be distracting during performance**.

Discuss this statement with reference to the management of your performance and with reference to how model performers manage these situations.

6

(d) Discuss how you can plan and manage your performance improvement in the short and/or longer term.

4

(20)

Question 2

Choose **one** activity.

(a) During your course you will have gathered data about **different aspects** of your **whole performance** in this activity. Discuss the significance of the information your data generated for **two** different aspects of your performance.

6

(b) Discuss how you used this information to develop a training programme to meet your identified training needs. For **each** aspect of your performance give specific examples of what you did.

6

(c) Describe how you managed your training **over a period of time** and explain any **changes** you made to your programme.

4

(d) Describe **how** your training influenced your ability to meet the **demands** of performance in your chosen activity.

4

(20)

SECTION 2: PREPARATION OF THE BODY

Marks

Question 3

Choose **an** activity.

(a) Describe the **methods** you used to assess your fitness to meet the demands of performance in this activity.

4

(b) Use your knowledge and understanding to explain the **principles** that underpin **progressive fitness training**.

4

(c) Discuss **one method** of training you used and the **advantages** it offered for developing a **specific type** of fitness for performance in this activity.

6

(d) Discuss how you applied the principles of training identified in Part (b) in planning and carrying out the training method you used. Support your discussion with specific examples from your training programme.

6

(20)

Question 4

Choose **an** activity.

(a) Use your knowledge and understanding to discuss why **one aspect of each** of the following **types of fitness** is needed for successful performance in the chosen activity.

- **physical fitness**
- **skill-related fitness**
- **mental fitness**

6

(b) Choose **one** of the **aspects** of fitness you identified in Part (a). Discuss your knowledge of **fitness assessment methods** in relation to this aspect of fitness and the information different methods can provide.

4

(c) Describe, in detail, the content of a **training programme** where you focused on the **aspect of fitness** identified in Part (b) to develop your performance.

6

(d) Choose **one** of the other **aspects of fitness** you identified in Part (a). For this aspect discuss your future training needs to further develop your performance.

4

(20)

SECTION 3: SKILLS AND TECHNIQUES

Marks

Question 5

Choose **one** activity.

(a) Describe some of the features of performance that can be identified at each of the **stages of skill learning**. Give specific examples from the chosen activity.

6

(b) Select a skill or technique from your activity. Give a **detailed analysis** of the features of **your** performance that clearly mark out your **current** stage of learning.

4

(c) When developing this skill or technique discuss how you used your knowledge of skill learning to design an appropriate programme of work. Give specific details of the programme you used.

6

(d) Describe how you evaluated the effectiveness of the programme you used.

4

(20)

Question 6

(a) Explain, in detail, what you understand about **information processing** and its relevance to learning and developing skill or refining technique.

6

(b) Select a complex skill or technique from an activity of your choice. When developing **or** refining **or** applying this skill or technique, discuss the **range of information** you had to process to ensure your performance improved.

4

(c) Describe, in detail, the **methods of practice** you used to improve your ability in the chosen skill or technique with a view to improving your whole performance.

6

(d) Describe, in detail, how you monitored your progress during practice. Explain what you did to ensure your progress was continuous.

4

(20)

SECTION 4: STRUCTURES, STRATEGIES AND COMPOSITION

Marks

Question 7

(a) Choose an activity and a structure, strategy or composition you have used. Describe how you **planned your practice** of this structure, strategy or composition to ensure you were prepared to **apply and adapt** it as performance circumstances required. **6**

(b) When using this structure, strategy or composition describe how your strength(s) and weakness(es) influenced your practice and performance. **4**

(c) Discuss how you **adapted your performance** in this structure, strategy or composition to reduce the effect of your weakness(es). Explain, in detail, the adaptations you made to minimize identified weakness(es). **6**

(d) As a result of the adaptations you made, describe how you evaluated the effectiveness of the performance. Identify **one** future development need within this structure, strategy or composition. **4**

(20)

Question 8

(a) Describe, in detail, a structure, strategy or composition that you would usually select as your **first choice**. Explain why you would select this structure, strategy or composition in preference to any other. **6**

(b) Discuss the importance of developing **alternative** structures, strategies or compositions when practicing to meet **less predictable** performance demands. **6**

(c) **During the application of a structure, strategy or composition focusing your attention on relevant information can ensure that effective decisions are made.**

With reference to the role you played **or** a performance you planned give examples of **two pieces of information** you would look for to help inform your decision making. **4**

(d) Discuss how you would organise your future training to ensure you had **opportunities to practice decision-making** when applying structures, strategies or compositions. **4**

(20)

[END OF SPECIMEN QUESTION PAPER]

[BLANK PAGE]

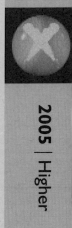

[BLANK PAGE]

X205/301

NATIONAL
QUALIFICATIONS
2005

THURSDAY, 2 JUNE
1.00 PM – 3.30 PM

PHYSICAL EDUCATION

HIGHER

Analysis and
Development of
Performance

Candidates should attempt **three** questions, each chosen from a different area.

SCOTTISH
QUALIFICATIONS
AUTHORITY

AREA 1: PERFORMANCE APPRECIATION

Marks

Question 1

Choose an activity.

(*a*) Discuss the **qualities** that you consider to be **strengths** in your performance.

4

(*b*) Describe how you planned to improve **two different areas** of your performance in this activity over a specified period of time.

6

(*c*) Describe how you monitored your progress during training. Explain the impact the training had on your **whole** performance.

6

(*d*) Discuss how you used **models** of performance to evaluate the development of **your** performance.

4

(20)

Question 2

Choose an activity.

(*a*) Describe how you obtained data about **two different areas** of your whole performance. What information about **specific development needs** did your data provide?

6

(*b*) Outline the training programme you planned to meet your development needs.

4

(*c*) **Justify** the relevance of the training you planned. Explain any adaptations you made over a period of time.

5

(*d*) Discuss the value of **setting goals** when planning training to develop your performance.

5

(20)

AREA 2: PREPARATION OF THE BODY

Marks

Question 3

Choose an activity.

(*a*) **Physical, skill-related** and **mental fitness** are all required for successful performance. With reference to your chosen activity, explain why **one aspect** of **each** of these **types of fitness** is important. **6**

(*b*) Choose **two** different **methods of training** that you have used (or have considered using) to develop **one** of the types of fitness discussed in part (*a*).

Discuss the merits that **each** method offers for the development of your performance in your chosen activity. **5**

(*c*) With specific reference to **one** method of training discussed in part (*b*), explain the importance of **progressively overloading** your training. Give specific examples. **5**

(*d*) Discuss the effects that your training had on your **whole performance**. **4**

(20)

Question 4

Choose an activity.

(*a*) Discuss why it is important to ensure that fitness training is:

  (i) specific to the **fitness demands of the activity**; and

  (ii) specific to the **personal needs** of the performer. **6**

(*b*) With reference to the specific demands of the activity, describe the **methods used** to make observations, and record data, about your fitness for performance. Briefly describe the development **needs** that you identified. **6**

(*c*) Outline a programme of work you used to meet the needs you identified. **4**

(*d*) With reference to your **whole performance**, discuss the effectiveness of your programme of work. **4**

(20)

[Turn over

AREA 3: SKILLS AND TECHNIQUES

Marks

Question 5

Choose an activity.

(a) Explain in detail, what you understand about the **principles of effective practice** when developing skill and/or refining technique.   5

(b) Select a skill or technique. Discuss **how you used** data gathered, and other information sources, to plan your performance development.   5

(c) Describe, in detail, a **programme of work** you used to develop this skill or technique. Give examples of how the **principles of effective practice** were applied in the programme.   6

(d) On completion of your programme, describe how your **whole performance** was affected. Outline what you would do to ensure your progress continued.   4

(20)

Question 6

Choose an activity and a skill or technique.

(a) What information about your performance were you able to obtain using one of the following **methods of analysis**?

  (i) Mechanical analysis

  (ii) Movement analysis

  (iii) Consideration of quality   4

(b) Describe, in detail, two different **methods of practice** you used to develop your performance of the skill or technique identified. Explain why you considered each of the practice methods selected to be appropriate.   6

(c) From the list below, select **two** of the factors that are **influential** in skill development. Discuss how **each** of the factors chosen affected the development of your skill or technique during practice.

  • **Motivation**
  • **Feedback**
  • **Anxiety**
  • **Concentration**
  • **Confidence**   6

(d) **"Skilled performers are able to select and apply the right skill at the right time."**

With reference to a **skilled** performance in an activity of your choice, discuss this statement.   4

(20)

AREA 4: STRUCTURES, STRATEGIES AND COMPOSITION

Marks

Question 7

Choose an activity.

(a) Explain why it is important to consider the demands of the performance situation **before selecting** a Structure, Strategy or Composition. Make reference to the factors you would consider.

6

(b) Describe, in detail, a Structure, Strategy or Composition that took into account at least **one of the factors** considered in part (a).

4

(c) Describe circumstances that required you to **adapt or change** this Structure, Strategy or Composition. Outline the adaptations or changes you made, and explain how they ensured your performance remained effective.

6

(d) Describe what you would do in the **longer term** to further improve your ability within the **original** Structure, Strategy or Composition.

4

(20)

Question 8

Choose an activity.

(a) Select a Structure, Strategy or Composition. Describe the **strengths** a performer(s) requires to apply this Structure, Strategy or Composition effectively. For example, you may wish to consider the physical, technical and/or the mental strengths required.

6

(b) When performing **in the activity chosen**, explain the importance of one of the following factors.

- **Group and team principles**
- **Choreography and composition**
- **Tactical and design elements**

6

(c) With reference to **the Structure, Strategy or Composition selected** in part (a), give specific examples of how the factor described in part (b) is applied to ensure an effective performance.

4

(d) Describe a practice/practice session where you tried to develop your performance **using the factor chosen in part (b)**.

4

(20)

[END OF QUESTION PAPER]

[BLANK PAGE]

[BLANK PAGE]

[BLANK PAGE]